French Notaires
and
Notarial Records
from the FGB

FGB

Anne Morddel

Suggested library cataloguing:

Morddel, Anne

French Notaires and Notarial Records from the FGB

Summary: Practical advice on using French notarial records for genealogical research.

[1. Genealogy. 2. France - History. 3. France - Law] I. Title

ISBN 979-10-96085-02-6

For my children

Table of Contents

Introduction

This booklet contains twenty-two posts from the first eight years of "The French Genealogy Blog"[1] on the subject of genealogical research using French notarial records. Some new material, including a glossary of notarial terms, has been written exclusively for this booklet. It follows on our first publication "French Genealogy From Afar"[2], which explains the basics of French genealogy and without which this booklet may seem a bit confusing.

The history of French *notaires* and the records they create is a huge subject and cannot be said to be covered in its entirety here. It is hoped, however, that this will serve as a significant and useful introduction to the subject and to the purpose for the creation of different types of records. It is our most sincere wish that you, Dear Reader, would find it of use in your search for your French ancestors.

---

[1] http://french-genealogy.typepad.com/genealogie/

[2] like this booklet, available from www.lulu.com

What Is A Notaire?

In French genealogy, the *actes d'état civil* -- the birth, marriage and death records -- are just the tip of the iceberg when it comes to finding out about ancestors. Once those have been found, the next area of research might well be the notarial records. For a few centuries, most French documents with any sort of contractual function will have been created by a *notaire*, but what is a *notaire*?

We will stick with the use of the French word *notaire*, rather than notary, for the two are different and should not be confused. A *notaire* is not the equivalent of a notary public, though the service of verifying a signature is one of the many things a *notaire* will do. Neither is a *notaire* a type of lawyer or barrister though, because they must advise on the law, they also study it. The sign represented above is the standard *notaire*'s shingle, the sight of which brings a sense of security to most French people, while the thought of a lawyer brings fear and suspicion.

Briefly, since Napoleon's *Code Civil* went into effect in 1804, a *notaire* is an official approved by the Ministry of Justice, but with his or her own practice. A modern *notaire* is required by law to give advice as to the law and the consequences of any document or transaction his or her clients may be considering. The documents drawn up by a *notaire* are official; they have probative force; they are enforceable; they can have the state seal. (Hence the sense of security in dealing with one. Gazumping by one's own *notaire* does not happen in France.) In Europe, this is known as the "Latin-style *notaire*".

Notaires existed prior to the *Code Civil* and served much the same function of drawing up and authenticating documents. During the pre-Revolutionary period, called the *Ancien régime*, they were known as *notaires royales*. Quite often their practices, called *études* (as they still are), and their authority, were hereditary.

In the past, many were itinerant, each wandering his territory and visiting huts, hovels and manor houses, writing out marriage contracts, wills and deeds. Do not think, however, that his lifestyle indicates a profession like that of some grubby little *épistolier* on the road. A *notaire* had robes of officialdom; even now, a *notaire* is <u>always</u> addressed as "*Maître*" (Master). To learn more about modern *notaires*, visit the site of the top training institution for *notaires* in France: the *Centre de Formation Professionnelle Notariale de Paris*.[3]

Notaires have always kept copies of the documents they draw up, called *les minutes* or sometimes, *les actes*, in their *études*. Forever. Through the usual little catastrophes that occur in this world, some have been destroyed, but thousands remain. Since 1979, the *études* have been required by law to turn over any of these copies aged more than 125 years old to the departmental archives. Most complied; some did not.

---

[3] http://cfpnp.free.fr/

Until recently, the only way to see notarial records was to visit the Departmental Archives, but more and more of the *Archives départementales* are filming these records and putting them on their websites. (Some of those that have already done so are Drôme, Hérault, Loire-Atlantique, Haute-Marne, Puy-de-Dôme, Seine-et-Marne, Var, Vendée, and Val-d'Oise.)

The study of notarial records covers a vast array of subjects, especially terminology, palaeography, and law, none of which we intend to pursue here. (We get bored with terminology unless it rhymes. We go blind with palaeography. Law intimidates us.) We will, however, give some basic information which we hope will allow those interested to make a beginning.

Notarial Records - Les actes notariés

The many interesting types of notarial records include marriage contracts, wills, guardianship arrangements, apprenticeship contracts, sales contracts, deeds, estate inventories, and records of payments linked to any of these. In them, individuals will be named, their appearances occasionally detailed, their relationships with others -- sometimes salaciously -- described, their disputes outlined, their accumulated belongings catalogued, their successes and failures clinically displayed. It cannot be denied; this is a bonanza.

The most genealogically useful of the standard notarial records are:

- **Marriage Contract**s, for they give a great deal of information about both families of the couple: full names of the couple, their ages (or at least a statement as to whether they had reached the age of majority), date and place of birth, current residence, whether either were widowed or divorced and the name of the previous spouse. There should also be the full names, professions and the residence of the parents and the witnesses. The dowry will be detailed, along with precisely how and when it was to be paid.

- **Wills**, for they name children, spouses, sometimes other relatives, and give an indication of wealth. Wills were very common at all levels of society before the Revolution. With the implementation of the Civil Code, the number of wills written dropped dramatically. Probably, this is one of the biggest differences in documentation between French genealogy and others, for in the U.S. or Britain, wills

11

continue to be left by most people, while in nineteenth century France, they are less common. The reason for this is that the Civil Code detailed and made law so precisely how estates were to be divided that writing a will became pointless. Only the tiniest changes have occurred in that law so it remains pretty close to what it was over 200 years ago. Essentially (and this chills the hearts of all the British retirees in France, in spite of a recent modification) the entire estate had to be divided equally between the deceased's children. No child could be disinherited. No child could receive more or less than another. There are dozens of points which prevent any sneaking around this and there are dozens more which detail -- to the sixth degree of relation -- who inherits what if there are no children or if they predecease. The point here is that the law was so clear that people just stopped leaving wills.

- **Estate Inventories**, probate inventories or, literally, inventories after death, however, continued as before the Revolution and became even more detailed after the implementation of the Civil Code. Since each child had to receive an inheritance of exactly the same value, there was an enormous amount of bickering about the value of every little thing. It is not at all uncommon for a family to dispute so much that the *notaires* will divide all of the deceased's belongings, all the contents of the house or farm, into heaps of equal value and tell the heirs to draw lots.

The inventory will contain the name of the deceased, age at the time of death, place and date of death, and marital status. It will give the names and ages of the surviving spouse and of all children, with their professions. It may also have attached to it all previous marriage contracts and payment documents to clarify the property ownership. The inventory itself is, of course, a fascinating insight into the possessions and lifestyles of long ago.

It requires doggedness to do so, but try to get the notarial records for each generation, for then it is possible to create quite a detailed history of the experience of the family, its economic ups and downs, many of its traditions, its little prides and great tragedies.

Array of Notarial Records

The array of notarial records is wide and really could be endless. People not only asked the *notaire* to make such documents as contracts, but to witness all sorts of ordinary or peculiar events. Working on a recent project, we have found much more via notarial records in relation to a family and all of its members than ever could be possible with civil and parish registers.

Notarial records are also terribly interesting to read and give a fine view on the lives and thoughts of the people involved. We occasionally buy personal libraries from garage sales, (*brocantes* in French), or second hand bookshops and have always taken pleasure in discovering the byways of the mind of the previous owner. We like meeting someone through his or her books. Going through someone's entire library gives a peek into that person's mind. Seeing all the books a person owned, which subjects are emphasized, which authors, which books are well-thumbed, which have inscriptions, which have been rebound, which barely touched, all of this gives a window on his or her interests, preferences, progression of thought. At times, we make friends with the long dead owner, have conversations with the mind that placed, say, a copy of Henry James's *The Golden Bowl* next to Guillermo Arriaga's screenplay, *21 Grams*. The experience of reading a number of notarial records for the same person or family can be rather similar.

Of course, they are not merely useful for gossip across the ages, but for genealogy. *Notaires* officiated over the drawing up of both family and business documents (perhaps explaining why the two are so intertwined in France). Below is a list of some of those most useful for genealogy, the time periods during which one can expect to find them, and what they could contain by way of genealogical information. It cannot possibly be exhaustive. All can be found in Departmental Archives, Municipal or Communal Archives or the *études* of the *notaire*.

- *Tutelles* or *curatelles*- guardianship agreements - can be found from the 16th century to the present. The actual judgment will be in judicial records; copies of it and of related reports should be with the *notaire*. The information they contain is: names of the deceased, heirs, minors, guardians, relatives of the minors and of the guardians, with their relationships, ages, dates, domiciles. This often involves a *conseil de famille*, a family council. (We have had the misfortune to sit in on a couple of these, which involved a disturbing amount of flying crockery.)
- *Emancipation* - emancipation of a minor being the documentation of the minor being granted adulthood before the age of majority - from the 16th century to the present. The information they contain is: names of the deceased, heirs, minors, guardians, with their relationships, ages, dates, domiciles.
- *Contrats de mariage* - marriage contracts - from the 14th or 15th century (depending on the region) to the present. The information contained: names of the spouses, usually the names of their parents, names of witnesses and their relationship to the couple, domiciles, professions, and sometimes places of origin.
- *Testaments* - wills - from the 14th or 15th century (depending on the region) to the present. The information contained: names and residence of the testator, heirs, relationships, and dates. Wills are often in separate books from other notarial documents. The reading of the will, however, will be in the usual, chronological book. This in itself is also useful, for the people who attend the reading are named and, for those who do not but should, addresses and professions are given.

- *Inventaires après décès* - Probate or Estate Inventories - From the 14th to the mid-19th centuries. The information contained: names of the deceased and the heirs and their relationships. There usually are two parts to the inventory: one of the deceased's possessions, the other of all their documents, titles, monies, shares, etc..

- *Partages de succession* - division of an inheritance - from the 14th or 15th century (depending on the region) to the present. The information contained: Names of the deceased, heirs and others present (e.g. husbands of heiresses), relationships, dates and domiciles.

- *Ventes* - sales - from the 14th or 15th century (depending on the region) to the present. Sales of property inherited will show the division of the proceeds among the heirs. The information contained: Names of the deceased, heirs and others present (e.g. husbands of heiresses), relationships, dates and domiciles.

- *Donations entre vifs* - donations inter vivos - from the 14th or 15th century (depending on the region) to the present. Often, these are the giving of property by parents to their children, but also between spouses. The information contained: names of the givers and receivers, their relationships, ages, dates, domiciles.

- *Reconnaissances* - recognition of a child - from the 15th century to the late 18th century. The information contained: the names of at least one parent, the child, dates and domiciles. In modern times, recognitions appear among the *actes d'état civil*.

- *Actes de respect* - formal requests for parents to give permission to marry - from the 15th century to the late 18th century. The information contained: names of the one who wishes to marry, the parents, the intended, their relationships and domiciles.

There are then the numerous business records which may or may not contain genealogical information: sales, purchases, rental agreements, debt negotiations, apprenticeship agreements, exchanges, receipts, and our current favourite: the *notaire*'s witnessing of a priest assuming his position as the new curate of a parish, complete with noting that he was led to the church altar, blessed, and that the bells pealed.

France is awash with notarial records. Take the plunge!

Actes Sous Seing Privé

A contract written by the parties and without a *notaire* at all is known as an *acte sous seing privé*. They are much rarer than notarial records and, in the archives, are treated similarly and stored with them.

Old French in Old Documents

Let it be known from the start that we do not enjoy old documents when they are illegible, any more than we enjoy attempting conversation with a person whose thoughts are incoherent. Language is about communication. When it fails, we are depressed. Puzzles are a different matter, being most intriguing, and language puzzles are quite enjoyable. Thus, in old documents, we groan at the sight of one that is nothing but a mess of scribbles and are rather excited to work with one that is legible but full of mystery.

In old French documents (here, we must qualify that "old" is really only slightly old, perhaps dating back to the sixteenth or seventeenth century, as few of us are likely to encounter anything much older in our genealogical research) there are two assaults on understanding:

- The handwriting
- The words

The handwriting has to be learned and that comes with practice. There are numerous books on French paleography. One in English that we have found helpful is Dawson's and Kennedy-Skipton's "Elizabethan Handwriting 1500-1650". Reader *Monsieur C* recommends "*Lire le français d'hier: Manuel de paléographie moderne XVe - XVIIIe siècle*" by Gabriel Audisio and Isabelle Rambaud, and a dictionary of Middle French: "*Dictionnaire du moyen française*" by Algridas Julien Greimas and Theresa Mary Kary Keane.

A few of the Departmental Archives offer palaeography courses. The best online course we have found (in French) is that of Stéphane Pouyllau,[4] and can be found on the website of Eric Voirin.[5]

For help with the old French words, we use Lexilogos,[6] the *ancien français* section. Then, there are the abbreviations used by *notaires*, which make no sense at all and are not even very consistently used.

Here are a few:

- nob for *noble*
- not for *notre*
- estt for *estant*
- led for *ledit*
- par for *paroisse*
- dem or demt for *demeurant*
- baill for *baillage*
- bo for *bon*
- cont for *contre*
- deff for *deffunt*
- dud for *dudit*
- fe for *feu*
- fre for *frere*
- R for *reçu*
- S for *sol* or *sou* or *sous* !
- succ for *successeur*
- susd for *susdite*
- test for *testament*
- tesm for *tesmoins*

_____

[4] http://www.stephanepouyllau.org/

[5] http://eric-camille.voirin.pagesperso-orange.fr/paleo/

[6] http://www.lexilogos.com/francais_dictionnaire_ancien.htm

There are many, many more, as well as some tricky little symbols for words. If you have traced your family far back enough to have many old documents to read, we suggest you take one of the courses.

Two Marriage Contracts

A Marriage Contract of 1791

The French Revolution did not happen overnight. Eighteen months after the assault on the Bastille prison in Paris, France was still in turmoil. The effects of the many changes were felt even in the deep countryside.

- Chateaux were being destroyed
- Tithing was abolished
- The salt tax was abolished
- Hunting rights were rescinded
- The Declaration of the Rights of Man and of the Citizen had been declared, granting freedom of religion, equality before the law, universal suffrage, equality of the sexes - in theory anyway
- Eighty-three departments had been created
- Paper money was introduced
- Church property was nationalized

In January of 1791, the Constitution had not yet been proclaimed and the Republic was more than a year and a half in the future. It was a time of uncertainty, and this is reflected in the marriage contract of Bernard LaMothe and Charlotte Teullet.

It was drawn up in the village of La Valade, near Saint-Avit-de-Vialard, in Dordogne, by the *notaire* Pierre Fourié, who was about thirty-five kilometers from his home in Molières. (This was at a time when *notaires* still went about from village to village, drawing up the contracts people needed.) The Republican Calendar is not yet being used, so he wrote the date in the old way as the "nineteenth of January, one thousand seven hundred ninety-one", and referred to himself as a "*Notaire Royal*".

21

The people to be married were Bernard LaMothe, owner and resident of nearby Pradelles (now the *Domaine de Pradelle*[7] if you want to stay there) and Charlotte Teullet.

---

[7] http://www.domainedepradelle.com/

The numerous witnesses included two men named Reymond Giry (Bernard's mother was a Giry) and Charlotte's mother and uncle. Her father was deceased.

They both agreed in the contract to bring to the union all of their goods, possessions, income and land rights, and that these and any more produced during the time of the marriage would go to their children.

The contract (the first page of which is shown in the photo above) is a copy made at the time, in which the *notaire* states that he affixed a royal seal [to the original] in the presence of all the above, plus further witnesses, Philippe Delpech and Jean Giry.

Then, all signed, except the bride. When the *notaire* asked her, she said that she did not know how to write. Fourié added that he was to register the contract before the twenty-fourth of January, which was presumably the planned date of the marriage.

As per the website of the Departmental Archives of Dordogne, the parish registrations for the town of Saint-Avit-de-Vialard did not survive in those turbulent times, though his death registration shows that Bertrand LaMothe did marry Charlotte Teullet (or Teulet). This marriage contract is the only record relating to the union and perhaps the only one naming so many relatives.

A Modern Marriage Contract

Firstly, let us remind all that a French marriage contract, historically, has never been a "pre-nup". A modern pre-nuptial agreement is a kind of insurance, meant to protect the assets of one or both parties should the marriage end in divorce. Marriage contracts have existed in France for hundreds of years. For most of that time, France has been a Catholic country, where marriages did not end in divorce. For the French, the marriage contract is closer to the British idea of articles of incorporation. Two individuals, members of different organisations, each with assets deriving from those organisations, are joining together to form a new corporate entity. Its success or failure was determined by its ability to produce and support and endow with assets new members. As we have written before: the French think of marriage the way Americans think of business.

Our example contract was written in 1901, on the ninth of September. The couple were married in October. The contract nearly always comes before the marriage. Sometimes, it may be the day before; we know of one that was written two years before.

The groom is aged twenty-six, a farmer, living with his parents. The bride is twenty-three and also lives with her parents. They are from neighbouring villages in Normandy. Both sets of parents are present at the drawing up of the contract. More, the groom's parents are "acting for him and in his name" and the bride's are "contracting the agreement for her and in her name, because of the donation they are going to make". The couple opt for the *regime dotal*, which groups together all that the wife is bringing to the marriage, either on her own or as gifts to her, into one category as her property.

The contract then goes on to list every conceivable type of possession the bride might have -- furniture, property, money, bank shares, railway shares -- current and future, and says that she will retain full rights over it all to do with as she wishes. She will also keep all of the income and her husband is not to touch it. The bride cannot touch the shares either, but only receive the income and she is to approve any expenditure of it the groom may wish to make. This absolute right extends to whatever she may inherit one day.

The next point states that she be allowed to make a donation inter vivos of any of her own property to any of her future children or grandchildren, without having to ask her husband's permission. Then, that the marriage forms a company in terms of acquisitions, each partner owning half of all, and that, when one of the couple shall die, the other shall have the right to usage (*l'usufruct*) of the home and all its furnishings exactly as it was, until his or her death.

The couple's individual belongings are listed. The groom has two suits, some clothes, underclothes and jewellery valued at five hundred francs, and he has fifteen hundred francs in savings, dear boy. His father is giving him a sum of seven thousand francs, once the marriage actually takes place, of course. The bride's parents are giving her a stunning trousseau: six sheets! Thirty-six blouses! Thirty-six pillow covers! Twenty-four tea towels! Forty-eight handkerchiefs!! A bed, mattresses, a mirror, pillows, nightstand, wardrobe, a parasol and an umbrella. The whole lot was valued at three thousand francs, and they gave her another five thousand in cash. (Note that the groom need not list in detail his clothing, but the bride's list details not only the house linen, but every one of her undergarments. Was this not embarrassing and humiliating, one wonders?)

People were modern in 1901 and there is a clause anticipating the possible dissolution of the company (not marriage) which states that the bride will keep all that she brought to and acquired personally during the marriage, especially her jewellery and any linens marked with her initials. However, should she wish, she may accept three thousand in cash if all has grown too tatty. The surviving spouse gets to choose from the communal property which bits will constitute his or her share. The bride gets to do the choosing if the company is dissolved. Should the company produce children, their inheritance comes from the community property, and the survivor's share is proportionately reduced, though he or she retains the use.

The *notaire* wrote that he read various and appropriate articles of the *Code Civil* to all present so that everyone knew the law. He gave the young folks a certificate confirming the contract, which they would then present to the *officier d'état civil*, who would have recorded the marriage. (He would note in the record that the marriage was under a contract, the contract type, date and the name of the *notaire*.) Everybody signed.

Although the wording refers to the rights and decisions of the bride and groom, it is clear that they had no part in the decisions as to the contract. In truth, in this case, even the groom's parents seem invisible. Yet, all in all, this is a fairly ordinary marriage contract, with many of the paragraphs being standard, as is the listing of the trousseau and even its price seems to be standard, hovering at three thousand francs for a good century. Perhaps one would dread meeting the bride's parents in court and perhaps forty-eight handkerchiefs is a bit much, but otherwise this is a good representation of how most French marriages began.

Defiance - the Acte de Respect

One thing we like about French law is that its approach seems always to have been to take all of the crazy things that humans do and make laws to deal with each type of behaviour. In this, some of their laws seem designed to bring people back into society after their little episodes of aberration, like roping wandering cattle back into the herd. Other countries prefer to deny that crazy behaviour is human or is normal, and try to stamp it out with severe punishment for each occurrence. This is comparable to shooting dead the stupid cow that wanders off.

The marriage contract above showed how much parents dominated the negotiations and decision-making. We felt sorry for the young couple, but at least their parents allowed them to marry. Here, we tell about what young people could do if their parents did not allow them to marry.

In short, they could each go to a *notaire* and have a Document of Respect, an *Acte de Respect*, drawn up. The *acte de respect* existed in the *Ancien Régime* (pre-Revolution) at least as far back as the 1700s, and continued into the nineteenth century as a part of the *Code Civil* (it no longer is). If parents refused to one of their children the necessary permission to marry the person of their choice, it was not necessary to poison people. The wilful child could start the process of gaining the right to marry without permission. To do this, he or she stated all the facts of relationship, address and age in the document, and then added that he or she was respectfully and submissively asking the parent to be so kind as to grant permission to marry. One had to wait a month for the written response.

It was hoped that the disapproving parent would say yes, but if the answer were to be no, the recourse was to issue a second *acte de respect* and wait another month. If the answer

27

were still no, then a third and final *acte de respect* and month-long wait was required. Then, the child could marry whomever he or she pleased. If the child were of the age of majority (twenty-five for women, thirty for men) before the process began, then only one *acte de respect* and a month's wait were necessary. Had they been in France, Romeo and Juliet would have lived, married, to a ripe old age, their passion and defiance smothered with the indifferent acceptance that so permeates that short but all-encompassing phrase, c'est *la vie*.

The *Acte de Respect* will be found in the notarial archives in the *Archives Départementales*. As it gives the names of parents and the intended, ages of those wishing to marry, sometimes the professions, and places of residence, sometimes with street address, it is a very good genealogical resource. It is priceless as a window on personalities and family politics.

A Guardianship Document Examined

It is incredibly cold and snowy in much of France just now. The document we plan to discuss reminds us of our early days here, struggling with the language. During a similar cold snap, down in the countryside, a kindly neighbour asked how we were managing, for the old stone farmhouses are difficult to keep warm. "Ah," we said "*Nous mettons une brouette dans le lit chaque soir,*" believing we were telling her we took a hot water bottle to bed at night. The neighbour said nothing, being polite or perhaps amazed, but her expression gave away that we had said something unusual. We asked if we had said something untoward. She pointed out the window into the garden, where stood a wheelbarrow, which is what we had actually explained to her that we took to bed, confusing *bouillotte* with *brouette*. With that, we sealed our reputation in the village.

Our guardianship document is about the Brouette family and their children and the arrangements made for their guardianship when Jacques Brouette died on his farm in 1760. He left two sons: Jean and François. His widow was Marie. His brother, Louis, was designated guardian, *le tuteur*, for his two nephews. This was something agreed by the relatives of the deceased after his death; it not being the norm for guardianship wishes to be expressed in life. (Bad luck, you see.) Louis was also to manage the deceased's property and goods for the children. (The widow being a woman, you see.) The agreement as to this guardianship, *la tutelle*, was drawn up by a *notaire*, signed by all concerned -- who had voluntarily gathered for the purpose.

A list of all of the deceased's possessions was then made and divided into three groups. Marie took one, for she inherited a third of her husband's estate. The relatives and guardian took another, for the same reason. The final lot was to be kept for the children until they should reach the age of majority (which was twenty-five at the time).

Attached to the documents is one dated seven years later stating that both Jean and François were adults and now could receive their inheritance. Their third of the possessions was listed again and they signed for them. At the same time, their uncle had to submit accounts for all the years that he was their guardian, *le compte de la tutelle*.

The entire document runs to thirty-eight pages and is a fund of genealogical information, for when the family gathered, it listed every person present, with place of residence and his or her relationship to the children. For the children, the widow, and the deceased, ages, dates of birth, places of birth and of residence are given.

As with other notarial records, they can be found either in the copybooks of the *notaire* who wrote the document or among the court records where it was filed, both of which will be in the Departmental Archives. Generally speaking, they exist from the sixteenth century to the present day. Among resources to discover the extended family of a person, the *tutelle*, if one exists, may well be the best.

Paris Guardianship Cases

Try as we might, none of us can hold back the waters of Time. We all go one day, some having prepared in advance for those who remain and some not. Genealogical research through the court documents of the cases brought about because things were left in a mess, or perhaps tidy but disputed, can be very rewarding. In fact, the more a family bickered in court, the more joy for their genealogist descendant. Doesn't seem right, does it?

In any case, since Paris research using the parish and civil registrations before 1860 is so difficult, any newly online resource on Parisians is welcomed with joy, even where it is evidence of sour relations between tions. The *Archives nationales* would seem to have been working toward winning some sort of award not only for putting records and indices to them online for people to use at no charge, but for allowing genealogists -- in controlled situations -- to do so as well. (We have seen them filming in the reading room, in their spiffy white coats and gloves.)

Recently available on GeneaWiki[8] are the guardianship records -- *les tutelles* -- for Paris from 1584 to 1791. Whenever a person died leaving minor (under aged twenty-five) children, a legal guardian had to be appointed. Normally, there was a family council to select an individual and the choice was reported to the court. The documents can name the deceased, the children, all of the members of the family council and their relationships to the children. Some of the files run to fifteen or twenty pages. These are incredibly valuable to the genealogist.

---

[8] https://fr.geneawiki.com/index.php/Accueil

This is a collaborative project. Volunteers have filmed the documents and put them online[9] in GeneaWiki's Paris section. Users are invited to index them. Also online is a partial index of some of the seventeenth century records, done in the nineteenth century. The documents themselves are in chronological groups, but for one, small section in alphabetical order. Thus, to be able to use this collection, you need to know when a person died in Paris to know where to begin the search. A few hints:

- The names of the deceased, the supplicant and sometimes the *notaire* representing the family are usually in the upper left-hand corner of the first page.
- *Succ^on* is an abbreviation for *succession*, French for inheritance. The identification of a case about the minor heirs of a Jean Martin would read: *Succ^on Martin*.
- M^e is the abbreviation for *Maître*, the honourific used for *notaires*. If the notaire for the Martin case were Lenormand, his name would appear below as *Me Lenormand*.

This is a truly fanfare-worthy resource.

Addendum: The images are uploaded by *Projet Familles Parisiennes*,[10] on whose pages one can find the nascent index. The images are hosted by geneanet.org. About one image in every two hundred is hopelessly out of focus.

---

[9] https://fr.geneawiki.com/index.php/Au_del%C3%A0_de_l%27Etat-Civil_-_75_-_Tutelles#Proc.C3.A8s_verbaux_1584-1650

[10] http://www.famillesparisiennes.org/

Two Wills

A Post-Revolutionary Will

Archives and records in France are termed as being either of the *Ancien Régime* or *moderne* (post-Revolutionary, e.g. from 1792 onward) and as the post-Revolutionary governments radically changed how many things were done, documents from the two eras can be quite different. Wills were no exception. Under the *Ancien Régime*, most people wrote a will and it was common for spouses each to make the other his or her sole heir. Older wills will contain a long prelude as to faith, requests and payments for masses and burial instructions before getting down to the nitty-gritty. From the early nineteenth century expressions of faith become less common.

The greatest change was caused by what has been mentioned here before: the rigid requirement of the Napoleonic Code, also know as the *Code Civil*, that all children of a couple receive exactly equal amounts. Portions of an estate may be left to others but primogeniture was abolished. No child can be disinherited; no child can receive more than another. If the child predeceases the parents and had children, his or her share is to be divided equally among those children. If a person had no children, then his or her estate must be divided equally among siblings, parents, and on to cousins. Hence the work of *notaires* in genealogy.

The will we examine here was written in Paris by the *notaire Maître* Jules-Victor Froger-Deschesnes, who owned the office, called an *étude*, number thirty-one (always expressed in Roman numerals) located at 47, rue de Richelieu, for twenty-two years. He had been in his *étude* for just a year and a half when he wrote this will for Dr. Pierre Delpeux on the 15th of January, 1822, which reads:

Before me, Maître Jules Victor Froger-Deschesnes and Joachim Cesar Perret, notaires in Paris, undersigned, and in the presence of Monsieur Cesar Joseph Jolinger, property owner living in Paris at no. 4 rue de Gramont, and of Monsieur Louis Mercey, hotel proprietor, living in Paris at no. 25, rue de Richelieu, both witnesses,

Appeared

Monsieur Pierre Delpeux, doctor, living ordinarily in Port-au-Prince on the island of St. Domingue, presently in Paris and lodged at the Hotel de Bretagne, no. 25 rue de Richelieu.

The said Mr. Delpeux being ill in body but well in mind has thus called the notaires and two witnesses undersigned and having been found by the said notaires and witnesses to be in a bed placed in an alcove facing a window in a room numbered ten, on the third floor, lighted by two casement windows looking onto a courtyard and being a part of the house in Paris at no. 25 rue de Richelieu called the Hotel de Bretagne, has dictated to the two notaires, in the presence of the two witnesses, his will which follows:

I give and leave half of all of my goods, property and letters of credit, without exception or reserve, which will remain on the day of my death to François Auguste Delpeux, my natural son, whom I have named [acknowledged] in the presence of these witnesses as my son.

I give and leave to Monsieur Haudandine, merchant of Nantes in the department of la Loire Inférieure, the other half of all of my goods, property and letters of credit, without exception or reserve, which will remain on the day of my death.

I charge Monsieur Handandine to pay on the half that I leave him of my goods the sum of two thousand francs to Elisabeth Delpeux, my niece living in Angouleme.

I name as my executor Monsieur Lemesle, merchant of Nantes, and I beg of him to accept this charge as a proof of his friendship.

I wish that the sum of two thousand francs which I leave to the named Elisabeth Delpeux will be paid to her free of all taxes and charges and I wish that these taxes and charges will be paid by Monsieur Haudandine from the portion that I leave to him.

I declare that I understand the bequests that I have made above to my son François Auguste Delpeux and to Monsieur Haudandine of all my goods, property and letters of credit, without exception which comprise my estate on the day of my death whether these goods be situated in France, the island of St. Domingue or elsewhere, without exception or reserve.

This will has been made and dated in the presence of the two notaires undersigned and in the presence of the two witnesses undersigned in Paris in the room designated no. 10 of the Hotel de Bretagne, in the year one thousand eight hundred twenty-two, Tuesday the fifteenth of January at ten o'clock in the evening.

The testator signed before the witnesses and the notaires after the reading aloud of the will by Maître Froger-Deschesnes in the presence of Maître Perret his colleague and the two witnesses. [All signed]

The wording and structure are standard for the time. The names, professions and addresses of the *notaires*, witnesses and the testator or testatrix are always given. If not in the *notaire's étude*, a description of the place where the will was dictated will be given. A person could also write his or her will and post it to the *notaire*, who would then keep it on file until the person should die, when it would then be registered. A confirmation of the registration will be put in the file with the original will.

Wills are good for finding family members, but for a view on the person's life as he or she lived it, nothing tops the inventory after death.

A Very Simple, Modern Will

We present here a very simple will from 1920, which is not all that different from one of 1822, examined above. Wills in France are usually short affairs. By law, a person must leave equal and set portions to each of his or her children -- including adopted but not stepchildren -- and this cannot be changed. Thus, most people simply add a few notes. If there are no children, there are requirements as to the relatives who may then inherit. (The European Union has just given a ruling allowing ex-patriates in France to bypass this law, which they find so evil.) If they have all predeceased the testator, as would seem to be the case of the will presented here, there is a bit of choice.

In November 1920, Marie Martin, a widow seemingly without children, in good health and of sound mind, appeared at the office of her *notaire* with four witnesses and dictated her will. She left everything to her niece, also named Marie Martin.

Du 24 Novembre 1920

Testament

par Madame *** Joly

ÉTUDE DE Mᵉ J. LAPIOS

NOTAIRE

MONSÉGUR (Gironde)

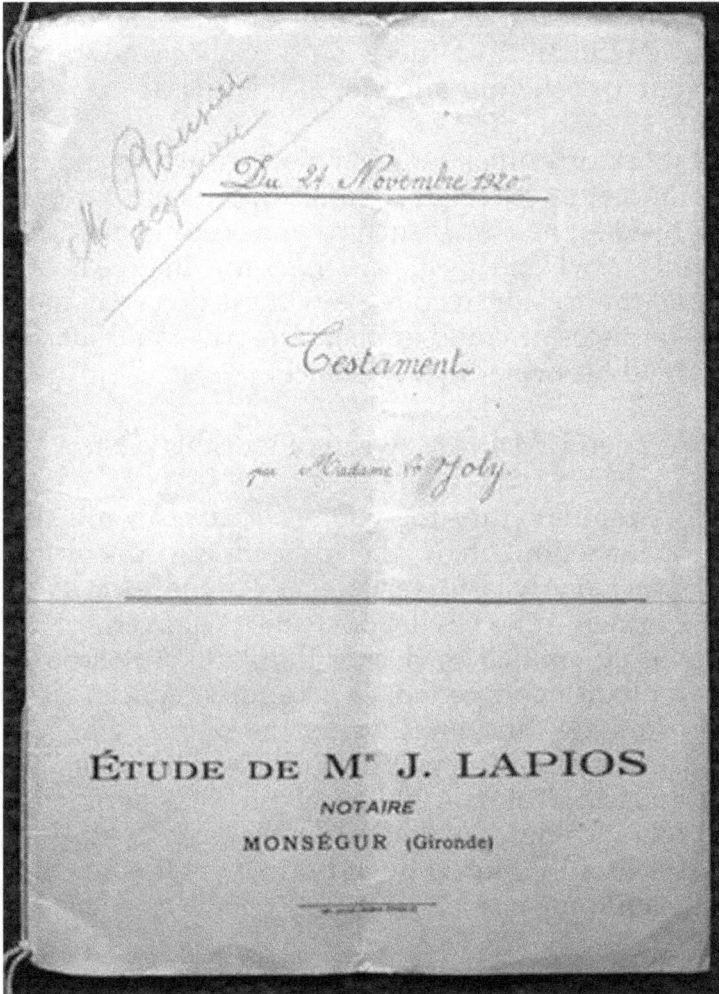

The beauty of even the simplest will can sometimes be the witnesses. They are not always relatives. Here, they are four gentlemen of various professions, all who live in the same town as the *notaire* and not in that of the testator. Perhaps she did not even know them; perhaps they were called in from nearby offices or workshops by the *notaire*. Perhaps in your genealogy research it is actually one of them you seek and not Marie. Unfortunately, few archives have put together an index of all people named in notarial documents, so there is no way to know in which document to seek your ancestor as a witness.

The best opportunities for such a search will come to those whose ancestors were in a small town that happened to have a resident *notaire*. If such be your case, we recommend that you trawl the *notaire's minutes* for the years during which your ancestor lived. As a witness or as a named relative, your ancestor could appear and you could learn much more about his or her real existence.

Our dear friend, *Maître* M. writes about this post:

> "A regular duty for young *stagiaires* in my day (we spent about half the time filing documents in the *greffe*, was to serve as a "friend" for a "Family Council". The Civil Code, since changed, required a family council to decide things like declaring your mother incompetent, or accepting legacies on behalf of minor children. Usually the *greffier*, who in those days carried the wonderful title of *protonotaire* (from ecclesiastical courts) had about three seriously close relatives but had to find four others to make up the seven minimum (I must find where this seven comes from some day).
>
> I have sent off old ladies to homes, told ten year olds that they must let their unknown to me uncle look after their property etc, with no guilt feelings at all until I read your note re witnesses."

Estate Inventories

Our outdoor thermometer puts the temperature at the moment at 40° in the shade at the moment, and our brain pretty much stops functioning at 35° but we shall endeavour to carry out our plan of discussing the value of probate inventory, or *l'inventaire après décès*.

Wherever an estate is to be divided or if executors simply think it expedient, there will be an estate inventory, *inventaire après décès, inventaire des biens*. It is performed by a *notaire*. All heirs must be present or represented. Normally, it is this listing of heirs and their relationships that give probate inventories their great genealogical value. But there is more.

The modern estate inventory, since 1792 at least, generally has four sections:

1. The, date, the place, and the identification of the *notaire*, the deceased and all those present
2. The listing, room by room, property by property, of all possessions and their value
3. The listing of all possessions on paper or documents, such as shares, promissory notes, IOUs, deeds, again with their value
4. The listing of all claims against the estate and their value.

The estate inventory of one Richard Ferris, (an Irish priest who rejected the Revolution's abandonment of religion, but accepted the end of celibacy by becoming a romantic partner and father, who spied on the French government for the English and stayed in Paris during the Restoration to run a Catholic college) runs to more than thirty pages. It was requested by his executors. In that of Lucie Cauchois, a wealthy Parisian woman of the eighteenth century, the detail and minutiae of possessions listed is endless, while that for Pierre Martin has a long list of his property deeds. All show claims against the estates.

While the list of possessions and the list of claims may show quite a lot about the personal lifestyle of the deceased, the list of document can be another part of the document to contain genealogical detail and also to lead to further research. It is here that one sees loans to friends and family, or companies that were formed or ended, shares bought in other countries, all property owned -- with names of those renting it, and all the other notes or letters the deceased did not want seen until after he or she were gone.

The Richard Ferris mentioned had few possessions, but his fingers were in many financial pies, as the documents list in his inventory shows; it goes on for many, many pages. Another man left a letter explaining that the reason an unknown young woman was named as an heir in his will was that she was reputed to be his daughter; though he did not recognize her, he was leaving quite a lot of property to her "out of respect for her mother".

Often, further notarial *actes* are detailed, giving the information necessary to find them in the archives and extend the research. With this, one can get those as well. It can be long and tedious reading, but the rewards can be very interesting indeed.

Probate Genealogy in France

In Article 745, the Civil Code of France states that, if there be neither spouse nor children who can inherit, then "collateral relatives beyond the sixth degree may not inherit", which has been taken to mean that said collaterals up to the sixth degree may do so. Article 716 of the *Code Civil* states that "the ownership of a treasure belongs to the person who finds it among his or her possessions; if the treasure is found among the possessions of another, then half belongs to the person who found it and half to the person in whose possessions it was found.

Et voilà! From these two articles, you have the birth of the profession of *la généalogie successorale*, French probate genealogy. How does it work?

Firstly, one must know how to determine relationships to the sixth degree as it is accepted in the Civil Code. Between the deceased and any relative who would be an heir, one must first find the common ancestor whom they share. One then counts the number of generations between the deceased and the common ancestor and between the potential heir and the common ancestor and adds the two together. If the result be six or less, a share in the jackpot is possible; if it be more than six, no luck.

For example: between an uncle who has died and a niece who hopes to inherit is the common ancestor of the uncle's parent who is also the niece's grandparent. The number of generations between the uncle and his parent is one; between the niece and her grandparent is two; the degree of relationship between the uncle and the niece is three. The niece is an heir.

Probate genealogists in France generally are contacted by *notaires* who find themselves with an estate that cannot be distributed, as heirs cannot be located. They must find all possible heirs and any legatees named in a will, if there were one. If they miss a single person who has a right to a portion of the inheritance, all distribution will be invalid. In their genealogical research, they may do the following:

- Beginning with the death registration, they find all relevant marriage, birth and death registrations of all relatives to the sixth degree.
- Will of the deceased's parents, grandparents and siblings are read, to identify possible heirs in the family.
- Military conscription lists, the *registres matricules*, are read to find any men or women who served in the military and to obtain more detail about them.
- *Recensements*, the census returns, are also examined.
- In a pinch, they have been known to chat up the neighbours for gossip, especially helpful in finding children born out of wedlock.
- As a last resort, they might use a private detective, but as the two professions are often at daggers drawn, this will usually only be to have the investigator find an address, never to allow him or her to become involved in the genealogical research.

In the above list, important differences in the *modus operandi* of the probate genealogist that are not followed by the family genealogist are:

- We try not to rely on gossip.
- We usually have no call for a private investigator.
- We usually do not have a *notaire* to gain for us the permission to see civil registrations that are less than seventy-five years old.

Speed is essential, for the law in France is that estates must be settled within six months of the death. Probate genealogists may, however, request an extension to that if they can prove that they are not dawdling but are truly hot on the trail of an heir or two.

This is an unregulated profession in France, but when questioned about it, probate genealogists assure one that they are *très sérieux*. Their work comes from *notaires*, who are regulated; and they take out professional insurance, which seems to us to be neither here nor there insofar as regulation is concerned.

It is an old profession, having begun in about 1830. It is also small, with only about one hundred probate genealogy offices in the country, employing about five hundred genealogists. It is also a proud profession, with its members seeing it as something along the lines of a paralegal profession and certainly not commercial. "You will never find us knocking on someone's door trying to sell a family genealogy tree," snipped one probate genealogist in an interview. Those trees, however, may appear in the documentation concerning disbursement of the estate.

The essential point, naturally, is the fee, which the unwitting heir must agree to pay (unless he or she were to renounce all claim to inheritance) before being told about his or her connection to the person who left the estate. It can range between ten and forty per cent of each heir's share (calculated after the taxes and *notaire*'s fee are paid), and up to sixty per cent if the estate be very large. According to our calculations, the remaining inheritance should rarely rise above forty-five centimes.

We are, lastly, stumped by the claim of the probate genealogist to comply with Article 716, for that hefty sixty per cent is more than the half of a treasure allowed by the Article. That same Article makes it very clear that the definition of treasure is "anything hidden or buried which no one can claim as his property and which is discovered purely by accident."

Did Your Ancestor Take Another's Place in the Army?

At the beginning of the summer, which seems so long ago, almost an age of innocence from this perspective, we wrote of the harsh demands of the French military during the nineteenth century. One of the ways for some to avoid serving was, of course, to emigrate. Another way was to pay someone to serve in one's place, to hire a *remplaçant*.

During the period from 1800 to 1872, the French Army permitted those called up for service to find -- or "buy" -- a replacement. The replacement had to be of the same age and he had to be approved by the recruitment bureau. If he were approved, the man being replaced had to pay something toward the replacement's uniform and equipment.

A formal approval of replacement might have been filed with the prefecture. If so, that would be found in Series Q in the Departmental Archives. Registers of replacements may be found in Series R. If a formal contract happened to have been made, that would be in the notarial archives in Series E (except for those of Paris, which are held in the National Archives.) Unless you have the name of the *notaire*, finding this last could be a long hunt through each *notaire*'s chronological list of acts written, his *répertoire*. It could, however, be worth it, in terms of rewards for your genealogical research, particularly if in Paris, where few of the military lists survive.

We came across a replacement contract of 1822 in the National Archives in Paris (carton no. MC/ET/960) in the notarial acts of *Maître* Grenier. It tells a tale:

Jean-Baptiste Amam (or Hanant), a gardener, contracted to pay Pierre Lablanche, a mason, to replace the former's son, Guillaume, in the army. Both young men were in the same recruitment list of 1821, but Lablanche had been released, while Amam's number was called. They said that there were friends. It was agreed that *Monsieur* Lablanche was to serve the full term -- with honour, no less -- that the army required of him. In return, said Lablanche would receive 1700 francs, in instalments, from Amam's father. There follow three pages explaining when and how the money was to be paid. Payment was to be made by "metal money only".

The contract does not name other family members, but it does give the addresses of Amam/Hannant and Lablanche. The call-up age was twenty, so it can be estimated that both young men were born in about 1801 and probably in Paris.

The different spellings of the gardener's name are an interesting secondary topic. Throughout the document, the *notaire* spelt the name Amam, while the man whose name it was signed it, Hanant. Neither version is at all common in France today. Why did the *notaire* insist on such a variant? Was it arrogance? Did the gardener have to present a document and, if so, was that the spelling on the document?

 That 1700 francs was quite a sum. Calculating monetary values across eras is tricky, but we have given it a shot using the website of Professor Rodney Evinsson,[11] of Stockholm University, which converts based on the value of gold. According to his site's calculations, 1700 francs of 1822 have the value of nearly 17,500 euros today. That would have been the full payment for six to eight years of military duty. Is that a fair price, do you think?

---

[11] http://www.historicalstatistics.org/Currencyconverter.html

Finding Notarial Records

Like many El Dorados, notarial documents are not always easy to find. To be quite honest, it is easier to pick a document and find the family to whom it once belonged than it is to start with the family and find their notarial records but then, that is the difference between the disciplines of history and genealogy, being the difference between the historian who can pick her subject and the family historian who cannot unpick Gramps.

To find a family's notarial records, if any survive, requires knowing the name of their *notaire*. This is because the documents are catalogued by the name of the *notaire* and the *étude*, in the *Archives départementales*, within series E. Normally, each archives will maintain a chronological list of the names of the *notaires* working in each area. If you know where your ancestors lived, you can then find which *notaire* was working in that area at that time. Then, it is just a matter of leafing through that *notaire's* documents for that time period.

Notarial records had to be registered. There are numerous *registres du Contrôle des actes* is in the *Archives départementales*. Unfortunately, they are not all in the same series. If the *notaire* is not known, but the date, place and family involved are known, it may be possible to locate the reference to the document in the *registre*. It seems that, across the country for marriage contracts, the *registre* (in series Q) is better for some years than for others: 1793-1850 is pretty good; 1850-1865 is said to be useless, but at least having *tables* - chronological indices; 1865-1904, generally also useless, without even having indices. (One begins to have the impression that *notaires* are a recalcitrant bunch.)

If there were a marriage contract, it should be mentioned, along with the *notaire*'s name, in any *acte de mariage* after 1850. If the name of the *notaire* is not mentioned, it's off to those tricky *registres*. If it still cannot be found, it may be possible to find the dowry payment documents - *les quittances de dot* - or a will later, with a copy of the marriage contract attached.

Finding a **will** is aided by the *Bureau de Successions*, an office where deaths were reported and logged. In many of the logbooks it will be stated whether the deceased left a will, along with the name of the *notaire* involved.

Finding notarial records is not terribly difficult; finding all such records for a family can be exhausting, but well worth the effort.

Répertoires

For every *acte* (contract, payment note, loan agreement, transfer of goods receipt or confirmation, will, probate inventory, marriage contract, promissory note, etc.) written in a notarial office or *étude*, an entry is made in a chronological list called a *répertoire*. The entry gives the type of *acte*, the date and the names of those involved. The *répertoires*, as these lists are called, make for dull but incredibly valuable reading. If you know that your ancestor had some sort of contractual agreement drawn up, which *notaire* he or she used, and the approximate date, you will be able to find it in the *notaire*'s *répertoire*. With the precise date from the *répertoire*, you are then able to request the correct carton from the archives and see the document.

Notarial records are normally kept in the appropriate Departmental Archives, however, those for Paris are not in the Departmental Archives of Paris but in the *Archives nationales* on *rue des Quatre Fils*. Paris was the first to put the *répertoires* online, on the *Archives nationale*'s *Salle des Inventaires Virtuelle* (Virtual Finding Aids Room), or SIV.[12] SIV is an absolutely brilliant way to search the holdings of the *Archives nationales*, but we grieve for the loss of the old *Salle des Inventaires*, which was a real room full of shelves of printed finding aids and is now an office. The books and printed finding aids have been transferred to a cavern of a room at the Pierrefitte site.

---

[12] https://www.siv.archives-nation-ales.culture.gouv.fr/siv/cms/content/display.action?uuid=Accueil1Root Uuid

Contrôles des Actes

From 1693 through 1790, notarial *actes* had to be registered formally with the administration of *Domaines* within fifteen days of being written. The register is known as the *contrôle des actes*. Notaires had to go to the registration bureau closest to their offices (*études*) to make the registration. From 1706 privately written contracts, (*actes sous seing privés*) also had to be registered.

The register gives the:

- Date of registration
- Type of *acte*
- An extract of the *acte*
- Names of the parties
- Name and address of the *notaire*
- Date of the *acte*

Many bureaux of registration maintained *tables* (indices) to the various types of *actes* registered. Examples include alphabetic indices of:

- Marriage contracts
- Inheritances
- Wills
- Property sales

The *tables* were maintained by the individual bureaux as each saw fit, so they are not uniform across the country or even within a department. Additionally, many have not survived. There is no master index to all of the bureaux.

Insinuations

Publication of any transfer of property by contract or *acte*, called the *insinuation*, was required by law from 1539. The *actes* were written into record by court clerks. Until 1790, these too were under the administration of the *Domaines*.

Registration of Notarial Records After 1790

In 1790, the Insinuation procedure was abolished and the registration procedure revised. From 1790 all notarial *actes* had to be registered within ten days of being written, if the *notaire* lived in the same place where his *étude* was, and within twenty days if he lived elsewhere. Wills had to be registered within three months after the death of the testator.

New bureaux of registration were created in each department and have been revised periodically since then. There were now three types of register:

- Le **registre des actes civils publics** - this includes all of the usual notarial records.
- Le **registre des actes sous seing privé** - this includes all contracts written privately, without a *notaire*.
- Le **registre de déclarations de mutation par décès** - this includes all transfer of property by inheritance.

Again, *tables* (indices) to some of the various types of *actes* registered were maintained. These vary from one department to another but generally include indices to marriage contracts, wills, property sales and rentals, and, especially, the Table des Successions et Absences. This last gives information concerning wills and the transfer of property by inheritance.

Hypothèques

From 1970, the functions of registering notarial records and of maintaining a public land registry were combined with the *hypothèques*.

Registers of the

Bureaux des Hypothèques

We have had quite a few happy successes in locating all of a person's heirs in France by using the registers of the *bureaux des hypothèques*. Literally, the word *hypothèque* means mortgage in English, but the function of the bureaux covers more than that. Much has to do with property taxes and there are many columns for figures and calculations in the registers under scrutiny here. As anyone who reads this blog regularly will know, columns of figures drive us to dizziness and nausea very quickly so, if we can have successes with these registers, anyone can.

The *bureau des hypothèque* is a registration centre of all land and buildings, the names of all owners, the taxes levied on the property, any laws and ordinances pertaining to it, any leases or mortgages concerning it, any transfers of ownership or leases or debts. (No title search issues in France!) The *bureaux des hypothèques* were a creation of the French Revolutionary government, to take the control of land out of the hands of the crown and aristocracy and put it into the hands of the new government. They were abolished in June of 2010 and replaced by a section of the tax authority, which carries out the same function.

It is the function of recording the change of ownership or names on leases or mortgages, coupled with another law, that makes the *bureaux des hypothèques* so useful to the French genealogist. That other law is enshrined in the Civil Code and mandates that, when a parent dies, no child may be disinherited and that all children must receive equal shares of the parent's estate. This was and is so rigid that many people did not bother to write a will. When there is no will but there is property, or even a lease, is when the registers of the *bureaux des hypothèques* can be so helpful: all of the children and the surviving spouse will be named in the register called the *Mutations par Décès* when the death of an owner or lessor is reported.

Each declaration must give:

- The full name of the deceased
- The place of residence of the deceased
- The date of death

Then, all of the heirs must be named.

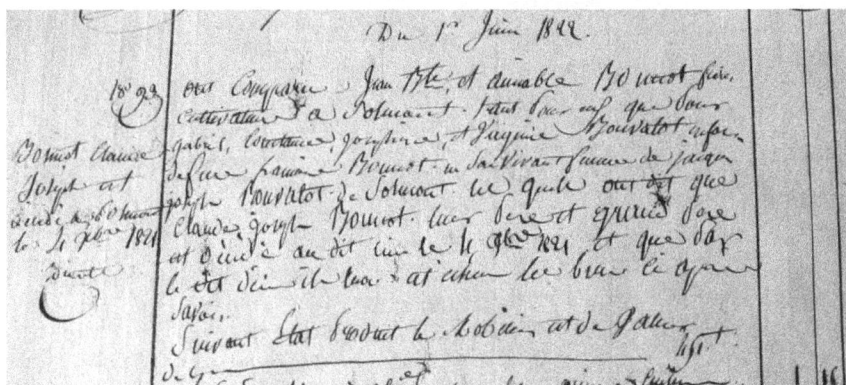

In the example above, on the first of June 1822, the heirs of Claude Joseph Bounot, who died at Solemont on the fourth of December 1821, made their declaration of his death at the *bureau des hypothèques* in Pont-de-Roide, Doubs. Roughly translated, the paragraph reads:

"Appeared: Jean Baptiste and Aimable Bounot, brothers, farmers at Solemont, representing also: Gabriel, Constance, Josephine and Virginie Bouvalot, all children of the late Françoise Bounot who, when alive, was the wife of Jacques Joseph Bouvalot of Solemont, and who say that Claude Joseph Bounot, their father [of the declarants] and grandfather [of the Bouvalot clan] died at the said place [Solemont] on the 4th of December 1821 ....."

Something of a jackpot in a single paragraph, *non*? Increasingly, the indices to the registers of the *bureaux des hypothèques* are being put on the websites of the Departmental Archives (listed with links in the column on the left of this page) so your ability to access them will get better and better.

How To Find a Modern Will

Finding a will or inventory such as those described in two earlier posts is not difficult if one follows the very precise procedures. There is a distinct process for recording *successions* (inheritances) in post-Revolutionary France. When a person dies:

1. His death is recorded in the local *mairie* (town hall) in the civil registrations as an *acte de décès*.
2. His death is recorded in the *Registre de Successions* (Register of inheritance). This also records if there were a will or not, and the names of any heirs. Later, the date of probate is added.
3. There is also a property book, the *Registre des Déclarations* or the *Registre des Mutations par Décès* (Ownership Changes due to Death). This will give the full amount of the inheritance, the names of the heirs, and how much was paid to each. It will also give the date and place where the will was made, and the name of the *notaire* who made it. This enables the location of the will, by finding the *notaire's minutes* (documents or records) for that date in the archives.

Look through the box and read the will to find if an inventory of the person's entire estate may not have been done.

Enjoy the hunt!

Marriage Contract Tables

Civil marriage registrations in the 19th century may state whether or not the couple signed a contract. If so, the name of the *notaire* and the date of the contract will be given. With this, you can go straight to the *notaire*'s *repertoire* to find the contract.

If, however, no contract is mentioned and there is no specific statement that none was written, it may be worth checking the marriage contract tables, the alphabetic index to the register of marriage contracts. These are found in Series Q in the Departmental Archives. Typically, the information that they will give includes:

- The full name of the groom-to-be
- His profession
- His place of residence
- The name of the bride-to-be
- Her place of residence
- The nature and value of any goods or property given as dowry
- The date of the marriage contract
- The name and place of residence of the *notaire* who wrote it

With this information, it is then possible to find the marriage contract, with all of its wondrous genealogical detail.

These tables work best when you have the knowledge from the marriage registration, e.g. the names of the groom and bride and their places of residence, as well as the date and place of the marriage. Without that, the hunt through the many tables would be too arduous.

For those not able to visit the Departmental Archives, some of them have put some *tables* and *contrôles* -- either for marriage contracts and/or for other notarial documents -- on their websites. As of this writing, they include:

- Cantal
- Charente-Maritime
- Drôme
- Hérault
- Loire-Atlantique
- Haute-Marne
- Puy-de-Dôme
- Pyrénées-Atlantiques
- Rhône
- Seine-et-Marne
- Var
- Vendée

So, for many, it may not be necessary to travel at all.

Follow the Trail to the End

Even though notarial records are not yet a heavy presence on the internet and so are not easy to research without visiting the Departmental Archives where they are physically located, we repeat that they are simply too valuable to ignore. The key reason for this is that *notaires*, being strictly regulated, were not at the service of their clients alone and could not draw up whatever a client may have requested; they had to draw up a document that was legal, with the identities of those named provable, which is why the collective word for such documents is *actes*. In many cases, identity had to be proven with copies of birth, marriage and death documents, or by witnesses, all details of which a *notaire* would note in the *acte*.

Too often, we research a particular generation of a family and do not branch out or continue up or down the line enough. This is understandable, for tracking all documentation of all in a line can be exhausting and, when the people are not closely related, suddenly and perhaps unfairly boring. However, we cannot recommend enough the taking of a dose of whatever provides courage and carrying on with the hunt, and we give here a case in point as to why.

For some months, we researched a family from Normandy, the land of cows, Camembert and calvados. Every member of every generation seemed to have produced large families. Finding out what happened to each of them called for a temperament both methodical and childishly optimistic. In the eighteenth century, they had acquired, a bit at a time, quite a lot of land. After the Revolution, none wrote wills, allowing the state to determine how to divide the property equally among all heirs. Some of these records survived and some did not; swathes were blown to bits during the Allied bombing of Le Havre in 1944. We doggedly paged through the indices to notarial records for the numerous towns and villages where the family lived, checking each document, however trivial it seemed, in which the surnames we sought occurred.

The document that proved a stunner of a bonanza was a sale of a patch of land by a great nephew of one of those we were researching. He was living more than a hundred years later than the period we were researching. He was the only child of a second marriage and the sole heir. He was not a farmer and he did not want the land. His father had inherited a part of it and had added more land to what he had inherited. Apparently, included in the whole were parcels belonging to aunts and uncles that his father had farmed for them, paying them a share of the profits. In order to sell, he needed to have their permission. In order for their permission to be of value, he had to show that they were part owners and how that was so.

As we turned to page two of the *acte de vente*, the sale document, we fell upon the family's genealogy outlined through four generations. Given only to show land ownership and the right to sell were:

- The names of the seller's parents
- The names of his father's first wife and their deceased children
- The names of all of his father's siblings and their spouses
- Where the siblings and spouses had died, the names of their children, who were the next heirs in line
- The names of his father's parents, from whom he and his siblings inherited
- The names of his father's grandparents, who had been the original purchasers

In all cases, dates and places of births, marriages and deaths were given, as were residences at the time of the document's writing.

This is the kind of work that explains why *notaires* have acquired impressive genealogy collections and why probate research still dominates French genealogy. It is what makes notarial records so wondrously treasured by family historians and so very worth the slog.

Overseas Notarial Records

The Archives Diplomatiques

The *Archives Diplomatiques* are in a fairly new site in La Courneuve, a suburb to the north of Paris and perhaps not the place to make this timid little archives-loving mouse feel safe. (Then again, there are those who feel the same about the wisdom of placing a NARA facility on the San Andreas Fault).

One takes the RER B to the La Courneuve - Aubervilliers Station, and then hikes under dark and gloomy railway flyovers to finally stumble down a wide pavement to the entry. Understandably, the security is rather like that at an airport. At the entry gate, one's bags pass though an X-ray machine and one's self passes blushingly through a scanner. Across a courtyard is the entrance to the building and we were directed to the *Salle d'Inscription*, where new users register and receive a little plastic, reader's card. Photo identification is required but registration is free.

From there, one moves to the usual type of locker room for storing all excess luggage, as only papers, cameras and pencils are permitted within the readers' rooms. Keep out your passport. The lockers are also free, a first in our experience. Then, there is yet another desk, where one must hand over the passport or identity card, the reader's card is scanned and a visitor's pass is issued. Finally, there is another security passage -- a turnstile -- with guard, that opens with the visitor's pass. From leaving home to this point took us two hours and we were ready for a cup of tea but there was none.

Why bother? It is here that one can find overseas civil registrations, personnel files of the diplomatic corps, diplomatic correspondence and, pertinent here, the notarial *actes des Chancelleries*.

The Actes des Chancelleries

All of those emigrants who left France did not always cut loose from their families. Many stayed in as close touch as the communication methods of the day allowed. They sent money home; they sent tickets for relatives to follow them. They were involved in the lives of those left behind. During the years of their separation, life went on as usual back home and it was, as usual or *comme d'habitude*, completely and thoroughly documented and certified by the local *notaire*.

Many times, a notarial *acte* was required from the overseas relative. As an example, for a minor child to be married, a father had to give his consent, the *consentement à mariage*. If he were in another land, he did this by going to his closest French embassy or consulate and asking the *notaire* or notarial substitute who would be on the staff there to draft the *consentement* for him. Written, witnessed and stamped, it would then be posted back home. And then probably lost over the decades. The *notaire*, however, kept a minute book, with an entry for each *acte* he wrote.

Other types of *actes* included *procurations*, or power of attorney, and confirmations of all sorts of things, such as deliveries and payments. According to the diligence of the *notaire*, the *acte* may have been noted in the minute book in a most cursory fashion or it may have been written out in great detail. We came across an entire contract copied into the minute book, taking up nine pages.

If the *notaire* were one of the more diligent, these minute books can be a superb resource for the genealogist. They often contain much family detail and can often be the best way to find or confirm a French immigrant's relatives.

The collection is entitled *Actes des Chancelleries* and covers the years from 1834 to 1900 (though not every consular post sent books for all of those years). The minute books were sent to the Ministry of Foreign Affairs by the various overseas posts each year. Initially, they were filed chronologically. In 1989, the archivists put them in alphabetical order by the name of the city where the embassy or consulate was located. (Beware of the article! The minute books for New Orleans, for example, are filed under the letter "L", for *La Nouvelle Orléans*.) They are not microfilmed and are not online. You have to go there, but it could very well be worth it.

Glossary of Basic Notarial Terms

A

- *Abandon* - In notarial records, to terminate an *acte*, to renounce a right, etc.
- *Acceptation* - To receive or agree to what is offered or proposed.
- *Accord* - The preliminary terms to a marriage contract.
- *Achat* - A purchase.
- *Acte d'apport* - The notarial act concerning the goods and monies that a groom brings to the marriage.
- *Acte de dépôt* - An act of deposit, whereby one party deposits something or a sum of money with another for safekeeping.
- *Acte d'état civil* - Civil registration of a birth, marriage, death, etc.
- *Acte de notaire* - Contract or document written by a *notaire*.
- *Acte de notoriété* - Notarial deed, affidavit.
- *Acte d'offre* - A document containing a formal offer (to purchase a house, for example).
- *Acte respectueux / acte de respect* - A formal request by a minor for a family council or parents to give permission for marriage, or for adoption.
- *Adhésion* - Adherence; commitment.
- *Adjudication* - The sale of a property or lease by auction.
- *Adultérin / e* - A person born of an adulterous relationship, also *enfant aldultérin*
- *Affinité* - Familial relationship by marriage
- *Agnatique* - In the male line, ascendant or descendant
- *Aïeul / Aïeule* - Grandfather / Grandmother
- *Aïeux* - Grandparents, ancestors
- *Aîné / Ainée* - Eldest
- *An / Année* - Year
- *Annuel / annuelle* - Yearly

- *Août* - August
- *Apparenté / e* - Related by marriage
- *Apprentissage* - Apprenticeship
- *Arrêté de compte* - Closure of accounts.
- *Arrêté de compte de tutelle* - Closure of accounts managed by a guardian
- *Arrière-grand-père* - Great-grandfather
- *Arrière-grande-mère* - great-grandmother
- *Assemblé de parents / Avis de parents* - The meeting and deliberations of a family council, held in the presence of a justice of the peace, to decide on issues concerning one or more relatives who are minors.
- *Attestation* - A notarised document whereby a person swears to the truth of something
- *Audit* - Abovementioned
- *Aujourd'hui* - Today
- *Avril* - April

B

- *Bail* - Lease
- *Bail à cheptel* - A lease of livestock, including terms for care and feeding
- *Bail à loyer / bail à louage* - A rental lease
- *Bail à nourriture* - Not truly a lease but more an annuity, a contract whereby one person agrees to pay an annual sum to another for upkeep or "food"
- *Bail à rente* - Lease of a building in perpetuity for an annual sum in money or produce
- *Bans* - Marriage banns
- *Baptême* - Baptism
- *Bâtard* - Bastard, illegitimate child
- *Beau-frère* - Brother-in-law or step-brother
- *Beau-père* - Father-in-law or step-father
- *Belle-mère* - Mother-in-law or step-mother
- *Belle-soeur* - Sister-in-law or step-sister
- *Billet à ordre* - Promissory note

- *Bisaïeuls* - Great-grandparents
- *Bornage* - The process of fixing boundary lines between properties
- *Brève* - The abbreviated, brief version of a notarial document or *acte*
- *Brevet* - A title or diploma issued by the government; also a patent
- *Brevet d'apprentissage* - Apprenticeship agreement or contract. The first party will always be the Master, the second, the apprentice

C

- *Cadet* - After a name or signature, second son
- *Caution / Cautionnement* - Deposit on a loan or its payment in full
- *Ce jourd'hui* - Today
- *Célibataire* - Unmarried
- *Certificat de vie* - Proof of life, certificate of existence.
- *Cession* - Ceding of a loan or a right; an *acte de cession* may also indicate the payment of a loan
- *Codicille* - codicil.
- *Compromis* - An act that identifies the arbiters on a contested issue
- *Compromis de vente* - A preliminary sale agreement.
- *Concordat* - The debt agreement among the creditors of a bankrupt person or business
- *Conjoint/e* - Spouse
- *Consanguins* - Children who share a father but have different mothers
- *Conseil de famille* - Formal family council to decide guardianship, marriage of a minor, etc., with the decision given in an affidavit.
- *Consentement en mariage* - The agreement of the relatives of a couple to their contracting a marriage This

is NOT an agreement between the couple themselves.

- *Constitution* - The formal act of constituting or defining something, thus:
    - *Constitution de cautionnement* - Definition of how a loan is to be repaid
    - *Constitution de rente* - Definition, or redefinition, of how a rent is to be paid
- *Contrat d'apprentissage* - Apprenticeship contract
- *Contrat de mariage* - Marriage contract
- *Convention* - The formal agreement of a contract
- *Cousin germain* - First cousin
- *Cousin issu de germain* - Cousin who is a child of a first cousin
- *Curatelle* - Guardianship
- *Curateur* - Guardian

D

- *De cujus* - The deceased person from whom a genealogical line, ascending or descending, has been traced
- *Décembre / X* - December / 10th month
- *Décès* - Death
- *Décédé / e* - Deceased person
- *Décharge* - The discharge of contractual obligations
- *Déclaration de grossesse* - A specific and legally required declaration of pregnancy, to be made by the pregnant woman
- *Défunt /e* - Deceased
- *Degré de parenté* - Degree of relationship - the number of generations between two relatives
- *Délivrance de legs* - The act of placing in the possession of an heir that which he or she was to inherit
- *Demeurant à* - Living in [a town or place]
- *Dépôt* - Deposit

- *Dimanche* - Sunday
- *Diocèse* - Diocese
- *Dit* - Said, but when it comes between names, such as in *Lebon dit Lafontaine* the word means "called" and that the person is called by a name added to or in place of his legal name
- *Domicilié* - Domiciled
- *Donation entre vifs / époux* - Donation inter vivos / between spouses
- *Dot* - Dowry
- *Dument* - Duly

E

- *Echange* - Exchange
- *Emancipation* - Emancipation of a minor.
- *Enfant* - Child
- *Environ* - About, approximately
- *Epouser* - To marry
- *Epoux / Epouse* - Husband / wife, spouse
- *Extrait* - Extract, statement

F

- *Famille* - Family
- *Femme* - Wife or woman
- *Ferme* - Farm
- *Feu / Feue* - Late, deceased (as an adjective)
- *Février* - February
- *Fiançailles* - Engaged persons
- *Fille* - Daughter
- *Filleuil / le* - Godson / goddaughter
- *Fils* - Son
- *Fratrie* - Group of siblings

- *Frère* - Brother
- *Frère germain* - Brother, sharing both father and mother
- *Frère utérin* - Brother, sharing the same mother but having a different father
- *Futur / Future / Futurs* - Groom / Bride / Wedding couple

G

- *Gendre* - Son-in-law
- *Grosse* - The copy of document or *acte* written by a *notaire* given to the parties
- *Grossesse* - Pregnancy

H

- *Héritier* - Heir
- *Hommage* - Solemn promise of loyalty to a lord by his vassal.
- *Homme* - Man

I

- *Insinuation* - An abbreviated copy of a notarial document or *acte* that has been formally registered with the relevant government bureau
- *Intestat / e* - Intestate
- *Inventaire après décès* - Estate inventory

J

- *Janvier* - January
- *Jeudi* - Thursday
- *Jour* - Day
- *Jugement* - Judgment
- *Juillet* - July
- *Juin* - June

L

- *Licitation* - Sale by auction of a shared inheritance
- *Lieu* - Place
- *Lieu-dit* - Name of a house or farm
- *Liquidation* - Liquidation, but also a clarification
- *Locataire* - Tenant, lessee
- *Location* - Rental
- *Lotissement de partage* - Division into equal lots the furniture and goods of an inheritance
- *Lundi* - Monday

M

- *M* - The abbreviation for *Monsieur*, not to be mistaken for a first initial
- *Mai* - May
- *Main levée d'hypothèque* - The removal of a mortgage, use as collateral, or any other limitation on property
- *Maître* - Master, an honorific title always used with *notaires*; abbreviated as *Me.*
- *Mandat* - Assignment of power of attorney
- *Mandataire* - Agent
- *Mardi* - Tuesday
- *Mari / Marie - Husband / wife*

- *Mariage* - Marriage
- *Mariage consanguin* - Marriage between cousins
- *Marié* - Married, husband
- *Mariée* - Married, wife
- *Marraine* - Godmother
- *Mars* - March
- *Masculin* - Masculine
- *Matin* - Morning
- *Mercredi* - Wednesday
- *Métier* - Profession, art or skill
- *Minute* - Original document or *acte* written by a *notaire* and signed by all parties
- *Mois* - Month
- *Mort / e* - Dead

N

- *Natif / native* - Native to or from a certain place
- *Neveu* - Nephew
- *Nièce* - Niece
- *Nom* - Name
- *Nom de famille* - Surname
- *Notaire* - A person who draws up all forms of contracts and documents, including wills and marriage contracts
- *Novembre / 9e* - November / 9th month

O

- *Obligation* - Contractual agreement to conform to the law
- *Octobre / 8e* - October / 8th month
- *Oncle* - Uncle
- *Orphelin* - Orphan

- *Ouverture de testament* - Opening of a will

P

- *Paroisse* - Parish
- *Partages de succession* - Division of an inheritance
- *Parents* - Parents; this can also mean relatives
- *Parrain* - Godfather
- *Patronyme* - Surname
- *Pension* - Subsistence payment, maintenance payment, alimony
- *Petit-fils* - Grandson
- *Petite-fille* - Granddaughter
- *Petits-enfants* - Grandchildren
- *Premier lit* - First marriage
- *Procès verbal* - Affidavit, formal statement
- *Procuration* - Proxy; power of attorney
- *Propriétaire* - A person who owns at least some land
- *Prorogation* - Extension
- *Publications* - Marriage banns
- *Puiné* - Penultimate child of a couple

Q

- *Quittance* - Receipt

R

- *Radiation* - Cancellation
- *Ratification* - Ratification
- *Reconnaissance* - Recognition, acceptance
- *Registre* - Register

- *Renonciation* - Renouncement
- *Rentier / rentière* - A person living off of passive income such as rents, dividends, etc.
- *Répertoire* - Alphabetical or chronological index
- *Résiliation* - Termination or annulment of a contract or *acte*.

S

- *Samedi* - Saturday
- *Second lit* - Second marriage
- *Septembre / 7e* - September / 7th month
- *Soeur* - Sister
- *Soeur germaine* - Sister, sharing both father and mother
- *Soeur utérine* - Sister, sharing the same mother but having a different father
- *Soir* - Evening
- *Sous bail* - Sublease
- *Sous-signé / soussigné* - Undersigned
- *Subrogation* - Subrogation, substitution
- *Substitution de pouvoir* - An *acte* by which an agent confers on another person all or part of the powers given to him or her

T

- *Table* - Index
- *Tante* - Aunt
- *Témoin* - Witness
- *Testament* - Will, testament
- *Transfert d'hypothèque / Transfert* - Transfer of ownership
- *Translation d'hypothèque* - An *acte* to make a change in a mortgage rate

- *Transport* - Conveyance
- *Tutelle* - Guardianship
- *Tuteur* - Guardian

U

- *Utérins* - Children of the same mother but different fathers

V

- *Vendredi* - Friday
- *Vente* - Sale
- *Vers* - About, toward
- *Veuf / veuve* - Widower / widow
- *Ville* - City or town